CONTENTS

ISBN-13: 978-1-4234-0795-9
ISBN-10: 1-4234-0795-4

Visit Hal Leonard Online at www.halleonard.com

HAL•LEONARD®
CORPORATION
7777 W. BLUEMOUND RD. P.O. BOX 13819
MILWAUKEE, WISCONSIN 53213

Away from the Sun

Words and Music by Matt Roberts, Brad Arnold, Christopher Henderson and Robert Harrell

I miss the life, _____ I miss the col - ors of _____ the world. _

_____ Can an - y - one _ tell _ where I _____ am? 'Cause

Chorus

now a - gain _ I've found _ my - self so far down, _ a - way from the sun _____ that shines _

w/ dist.

1.

_____ in - to _____ the dark - est place. _ I'm so far down, _ a - way from the sun _____ a - gain. _

3

A - way from the sun _____ a - gain. _____

so far down, _ a - way from the sun _____ that shines _ to light _ the way _ for me _____ to

find my way _____ back in - to the arms _____ that care _____ a - bout _ the one's like me. _ I'm

Duck and Run

Words and Music by Matt Roberts, Brad Arnold, Christopher Henderson and Robert Harrell

Intro

Moderate Rock ♩ = 86

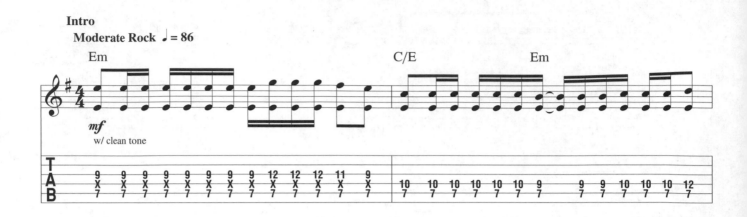

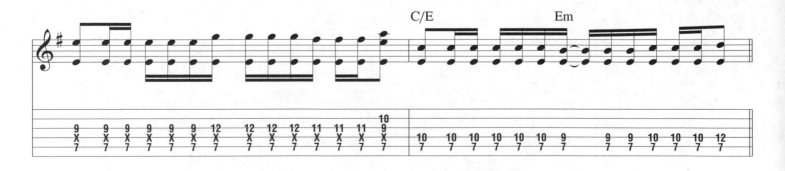

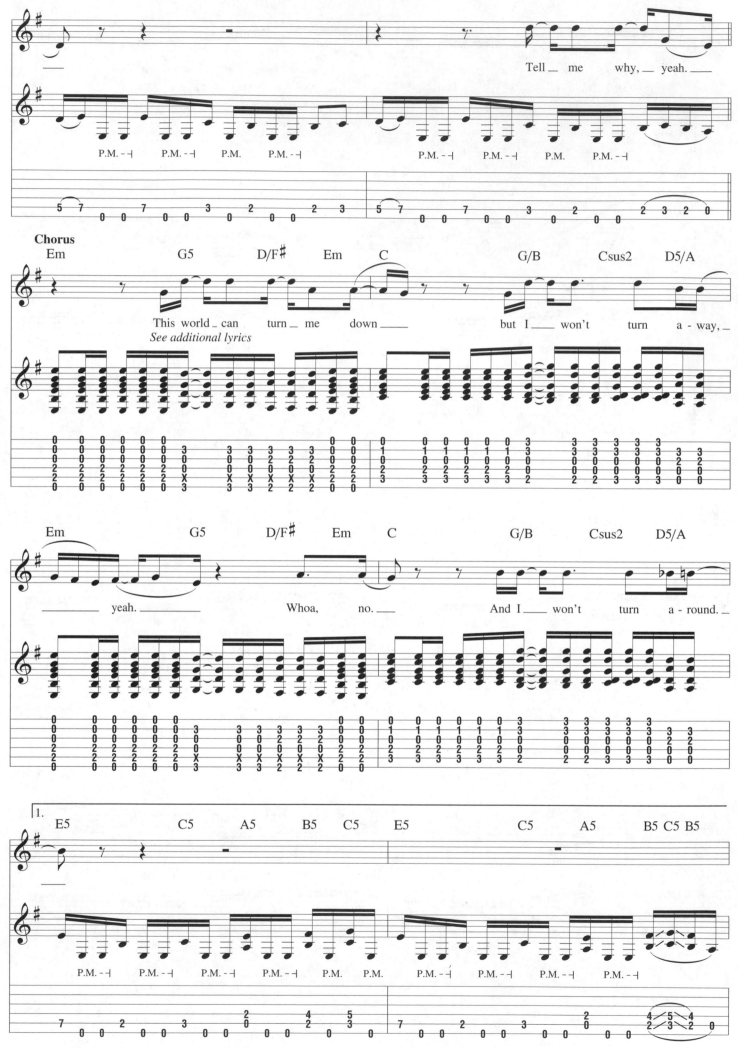

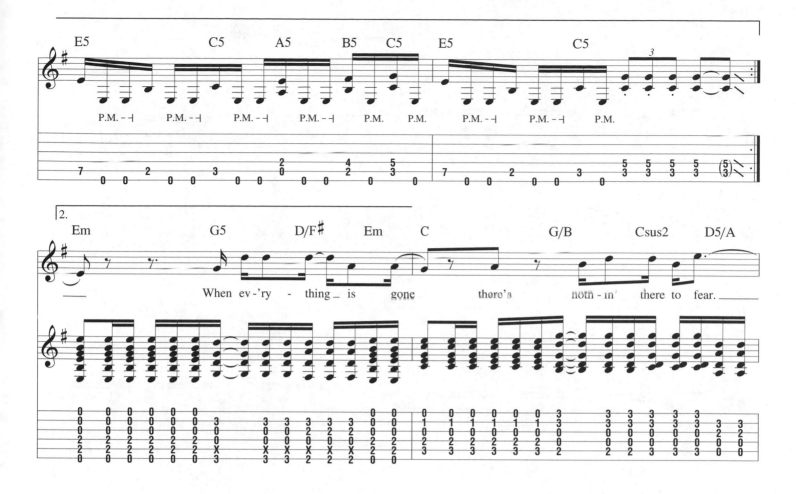

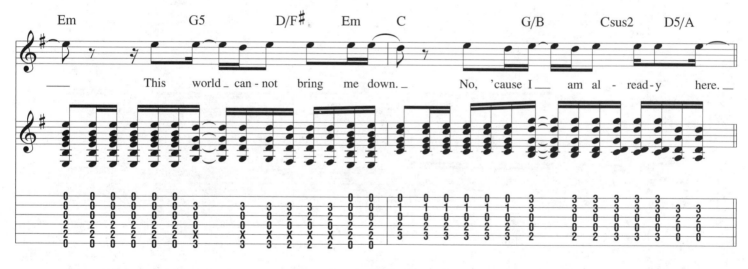

Bridge

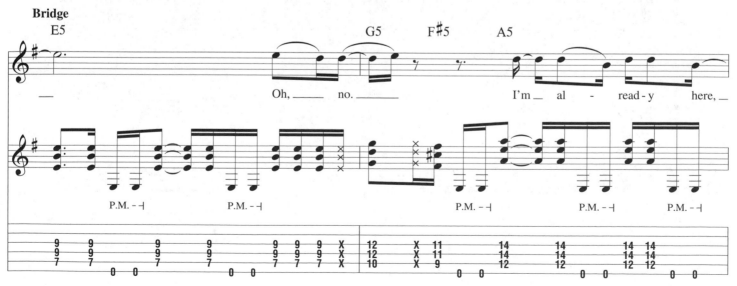

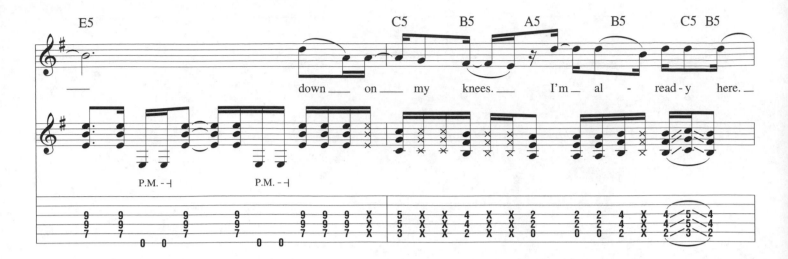

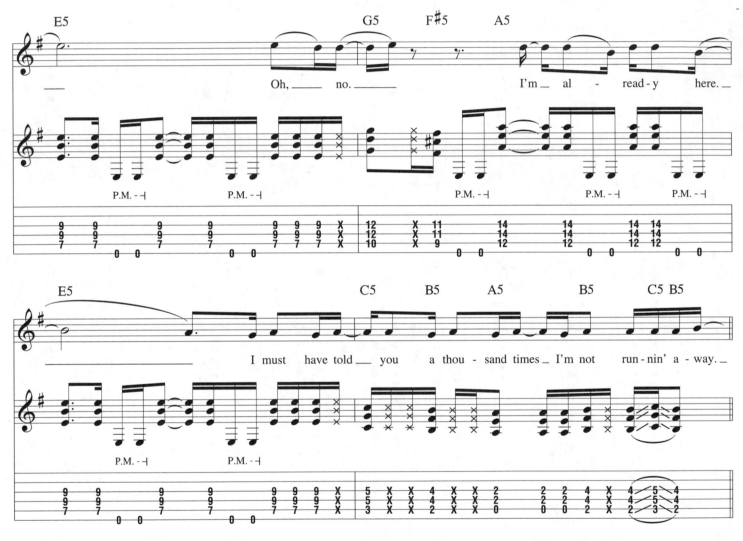

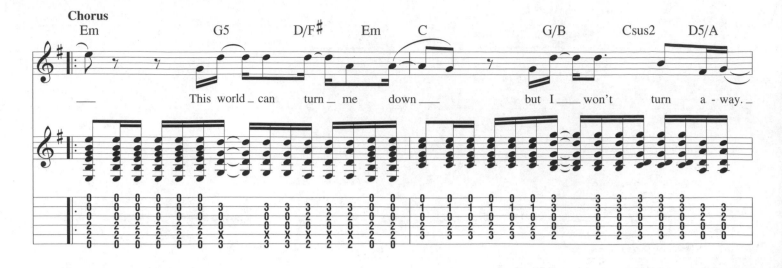

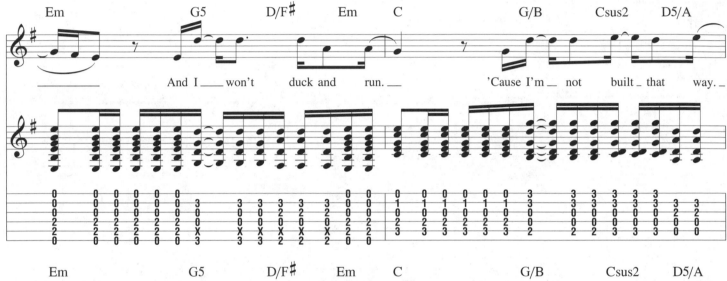

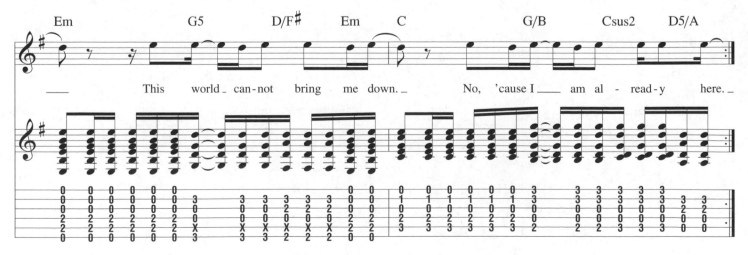

Outro

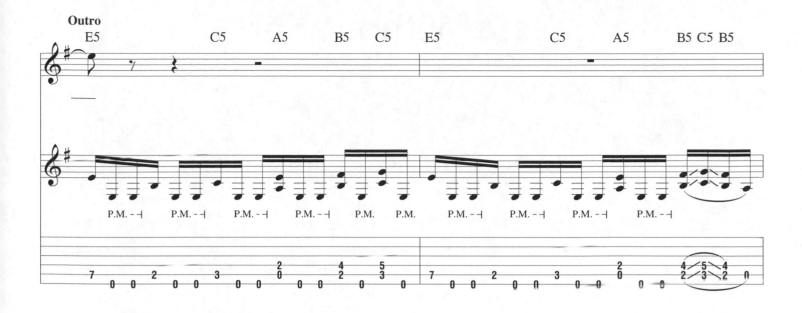

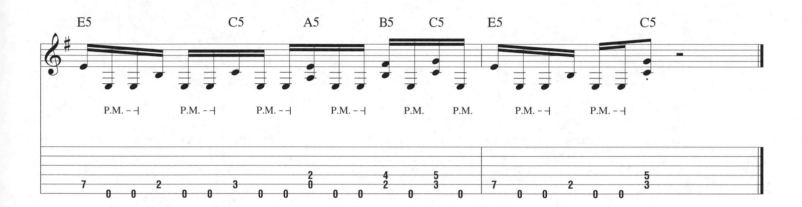

Additional Lyrics

2. All my work and endless measures
   Never seem to get me very far.
   Walk a mile just to move an inch now,
   Even though I'm tryin' so damn hard.
   I'm tryin' so hard.

Chorus This world can turn me down, but I won't turn away.
   And I won't duck and run, 'cause I'm not built that way.
   When ev'rything is gone, there's nothin' there to fear.
   This world cannot bring me down. No, 'cause I am already here.

Here Without You

Words and Music by Matt Roberts, Brad Arnold, Christopher Henderson and Robert Harrell

Tune down 1/2 step:
(low to high) Eb-Ab-Db-Gb-Bb-Eb

Intro

Moderately slow ♩ = 72

Bm   Bsus2   Bm   G   A

mf

let ring throughout

1. A hun - dred

Verse

Bm   Bsus2   Bm   A   Asus4 A

days have made _ me old - er _ since the last _ time that _ I saw _ your _ pret - ty face. _

Bm   Bsus2   Bm   G   A

_ A thou - sand

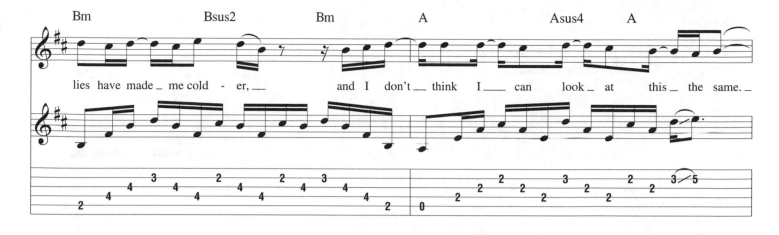

lies have made _ me cold - er, ___ and I don't _ think I _ can look _ at this _ the same. _

But all the miles _ that sep - a - rate, _____

they dis - ap - pear _ now when I'm dream - in' of _ your face. _

Chorus

I'm here with-out __ you, ba - by, but you're still on __ my lone - ly mind. __

__ I think a - bout __ you, ba - by, and I dream a - bout __ you all __ the time. __

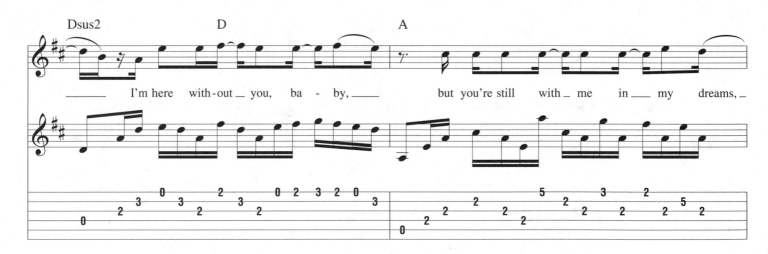

_____ I'm here with-out __ you, ba - by, __ but you're still with __ me in __ my dreams, __

__ and to - night, __ there's on - ly __ you and me, __

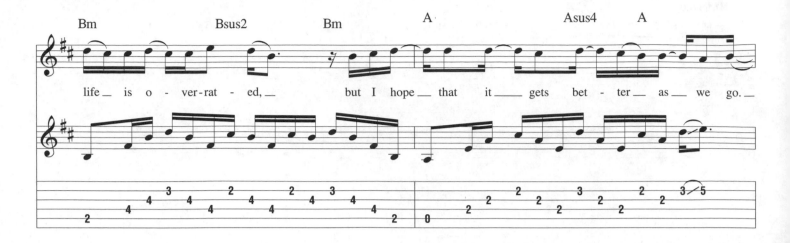

Chorus

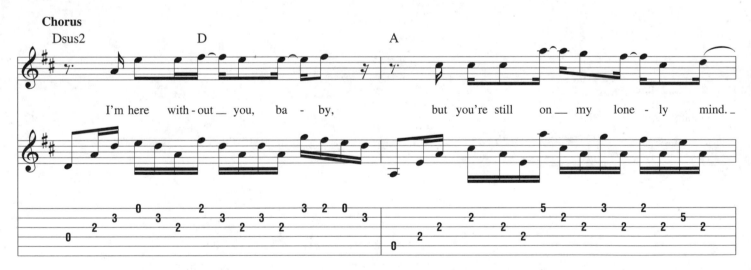

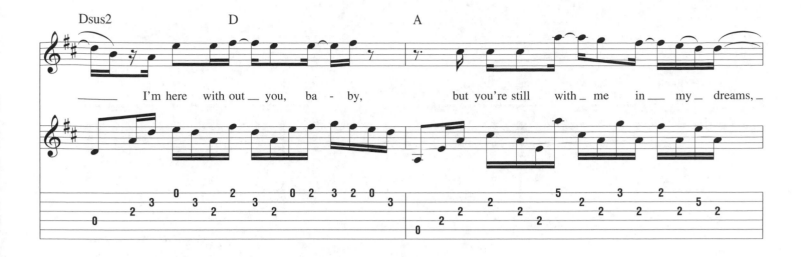

I'm here with out ___ you, ba - by, but you're still with ___ me in ___ my ___ dreams, ___

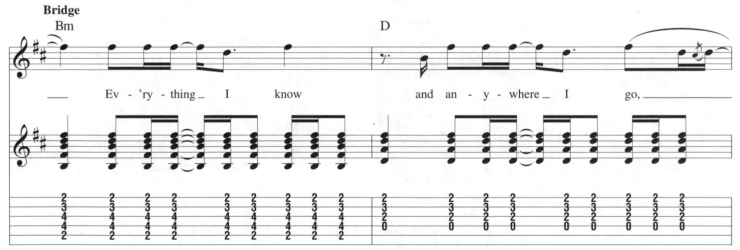

___ and to - night, ___ girl, ___ there's on - ly ___ you ___ and me. ___

Bridge

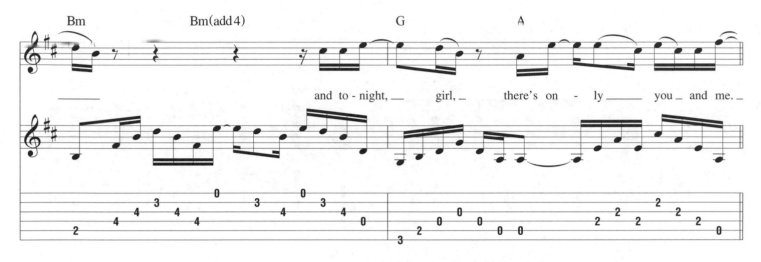

___ Ev - 'ry - thing ___ I know and an - y - where ___ I go, ___

___ it gets hard ___ but it ___ won't take ___ a - way ___ my love. ___

And when the last ___ one falls, when it's all ___ said and done, ___

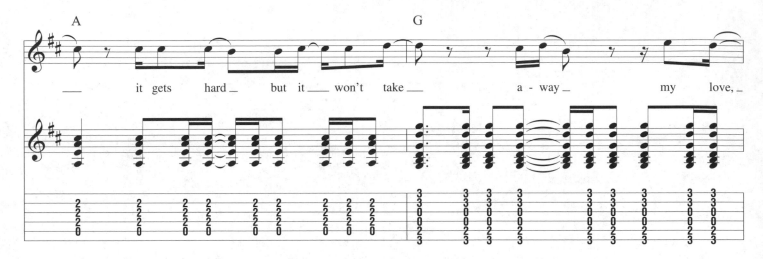

___ it gets hard ___ but it ___ won't take ___ a - way ___ my love, ___

Interlude

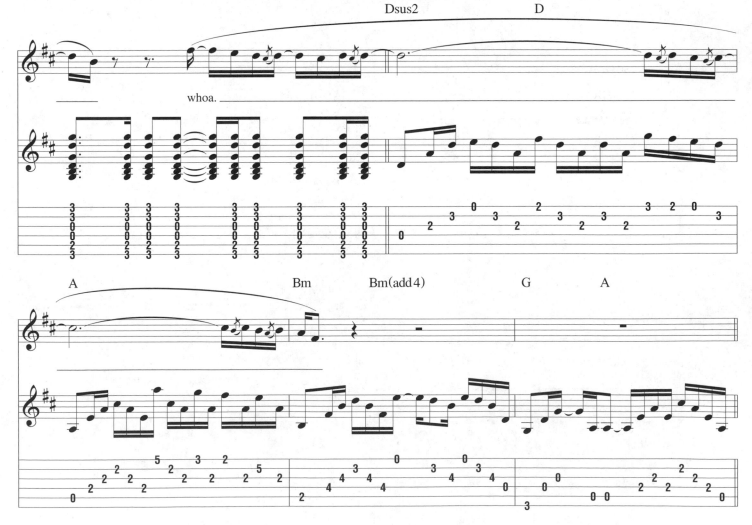

whoa. ___

Chorus

Outro

yeah.   Oh, _____ yeah.

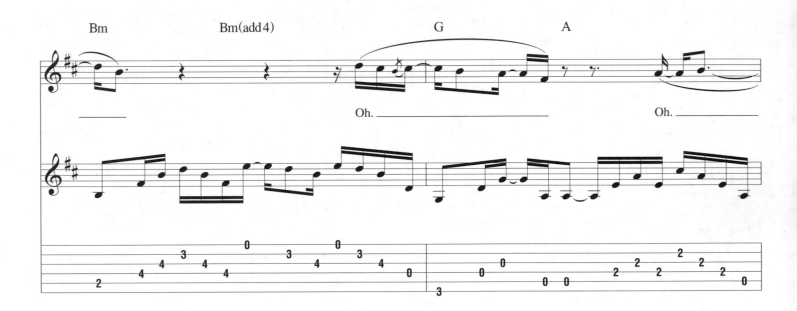

Oh.   Oh.

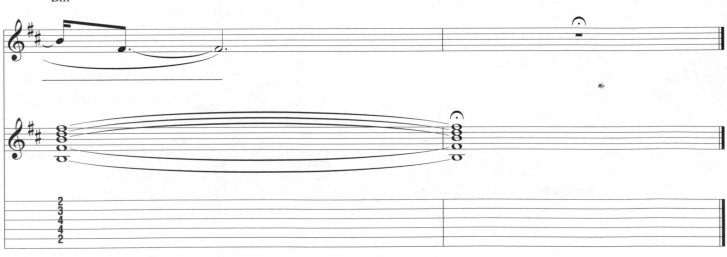

Loser

Words and Music by Matt Roberts, Brad Arnold and Robert Harrell

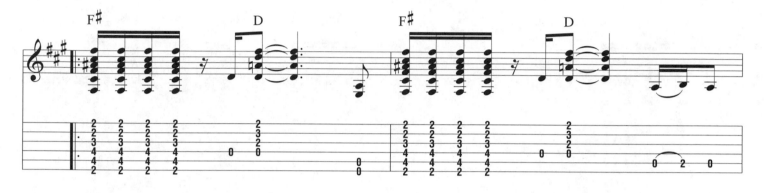

1. Breathe in right a - way,____ noth - in' seems__ to fill this__ place.__ I
2. *See additional lyrics*

need this ev-'ry - time. ___ So take your lies, ___ get off my ___ case. ___

Some - day I will find ___ a love that flows ___ through me like ___ this. ___ And

this will fall a - way. ___ This will fall a - way. ___

𝄋 Chorus

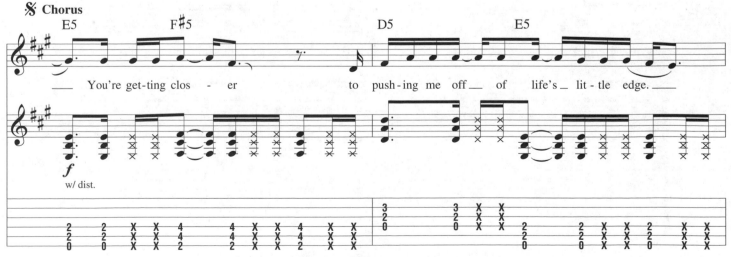

___ You're get-ting clos - er to push-ing me off ___ of life's ___ lit - tle edge. ___

f
w/ dist.

24

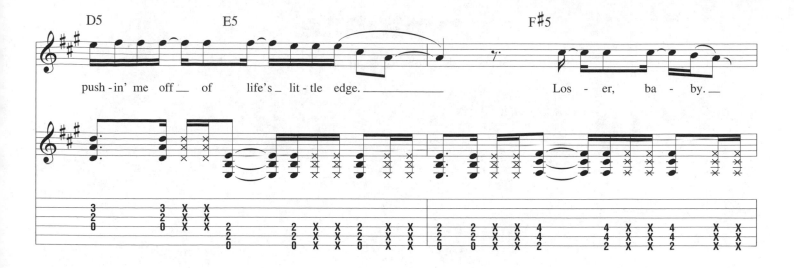

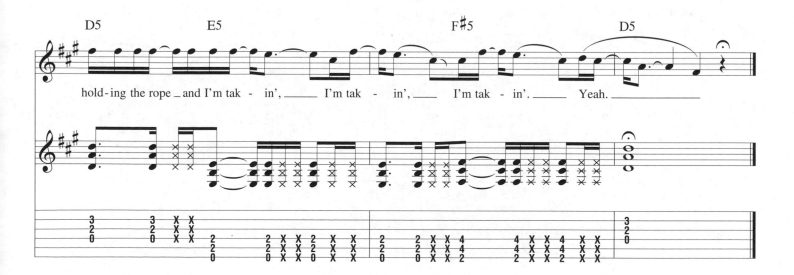

Additional Lyrics

2. This is getting old.
   I can't break these chains that I hold.
   My body's growin' cold.
   There's nothing left of this mind or my soul.
   Addiction needs a pacifier.
   The buzz of this poison is taking me higher.
   And this will fall away. This will fall away.

Kryptonite

Words and Music by Matt Roberts, Brad Arnold and Todd Harrell

Intro
Moderately slow Rock ♩ = 120

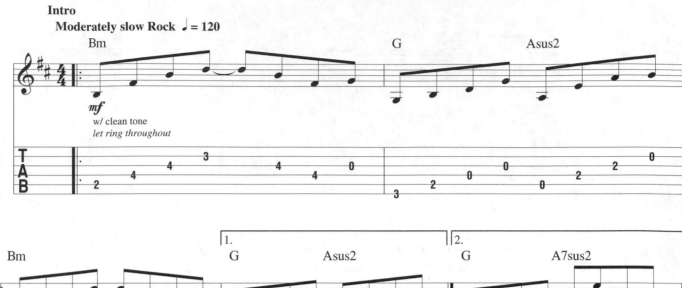

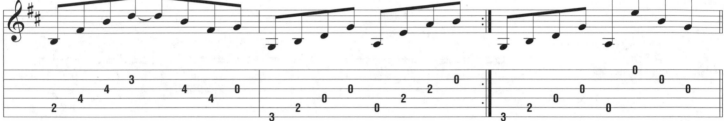

Verse

1. Well, I took a walk around the world to ease my troubled mind.

I left my body lying somewhere in the sands of time.

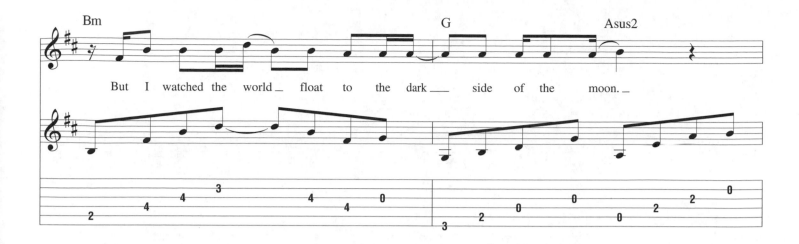

But I watched the world ___ float to the dark ___ side of the moon. ___

I feel there's noth-ing I ____ can do. ____ Yeah. ___

Interlude

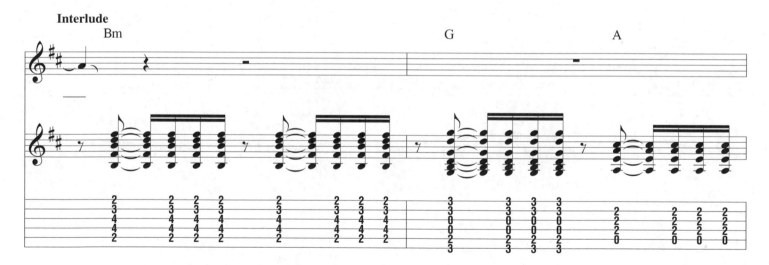

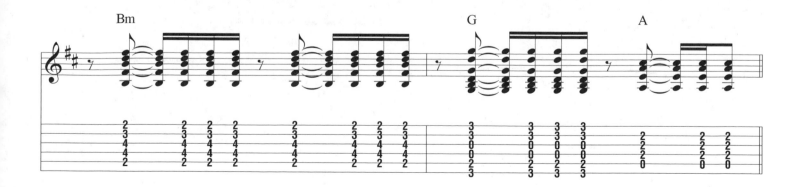

Verse

2. I watched the world float to the dark side of the moon.
3. *See additional lyrics*

Af-ter all, I knew it had to be some-thing to do with you.

*3rd time, bass plays E. **3rd time, bass plays F#.

I real-ly don't mind what hap-pens now and then, as

long as you'll be my friend at the end.

***3rd time, as before.

§ **Chorus**

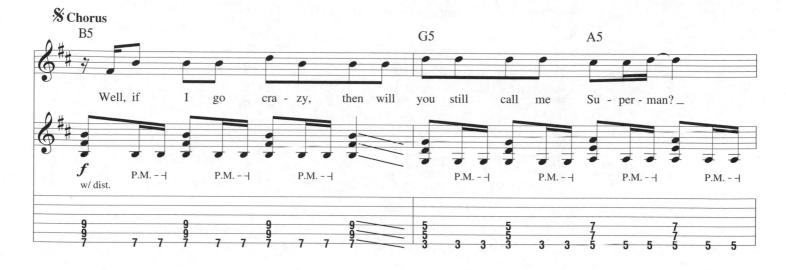

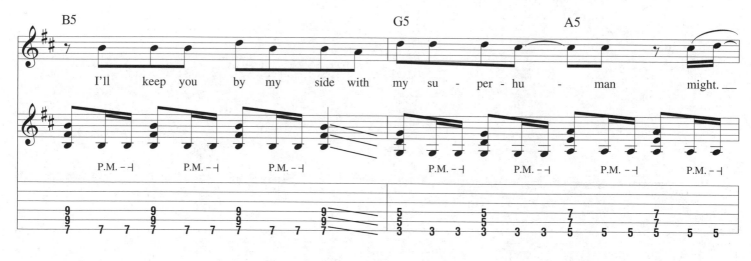

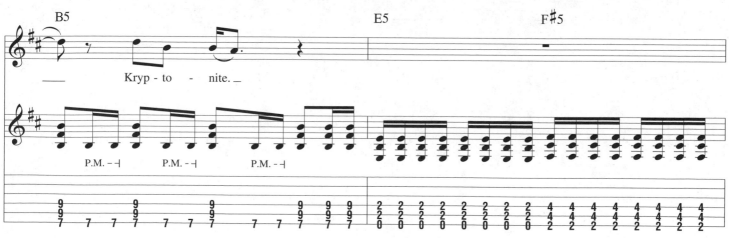

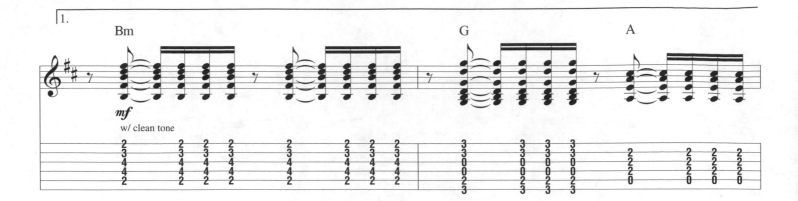

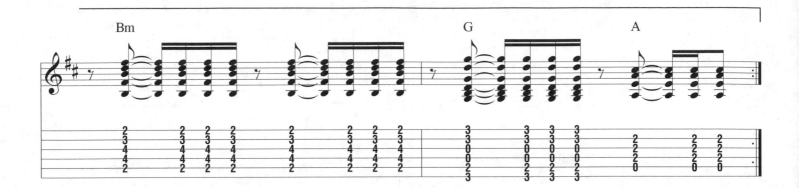

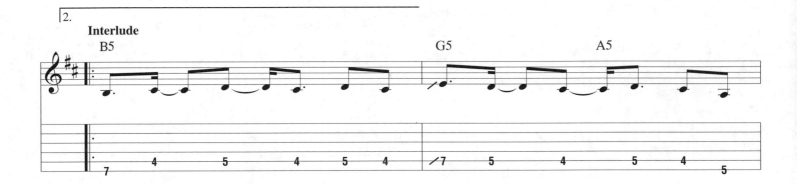

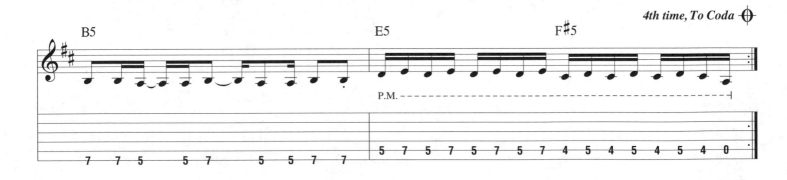

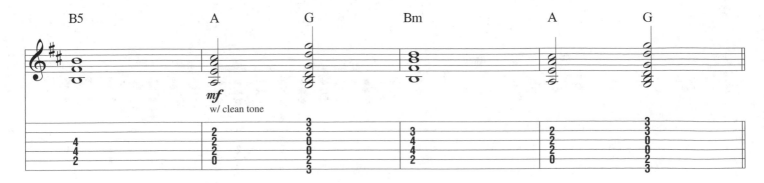

32

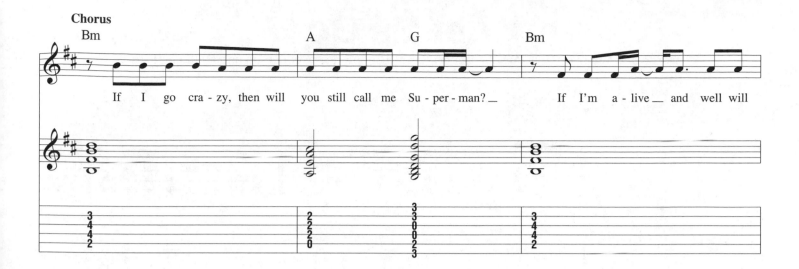

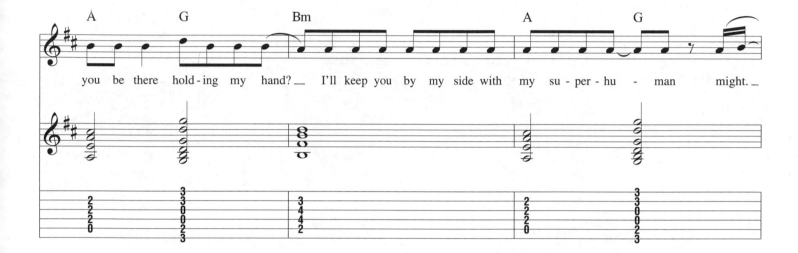

Additional Lyrics

3. You called me strong, you called me weak,
   But still your secrets I will keep.
   You took for granted all the times I never let you down.
   You stumbled in and bumped your head.
   If not for me, then you'd be dead.
   I picked you up and put you back on solid ground.

Let Me Go

Words and Music by Brad Arnold, Robert Harrell, Christopher Henderson and Matthew Roberts

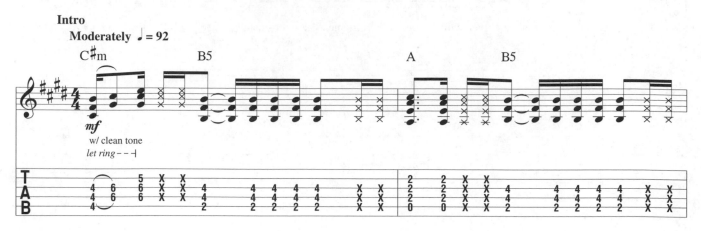

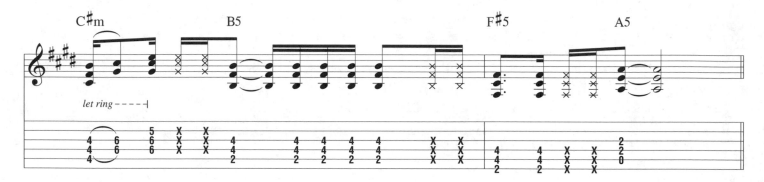

1. One more kiss could be the best thing,
2. *See additional lyrics*

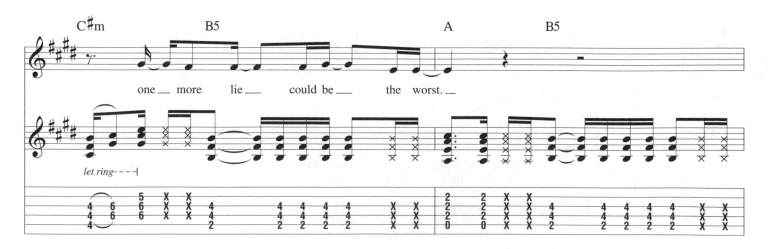

one more lie could be the worst.

And all ___ these thoughts ___ are nev-er rest - ing

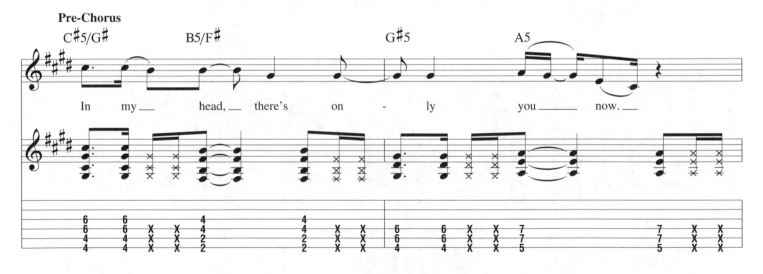

and you're ___ not some - thin' I ___ de - serve. ___

Pre-Chorus

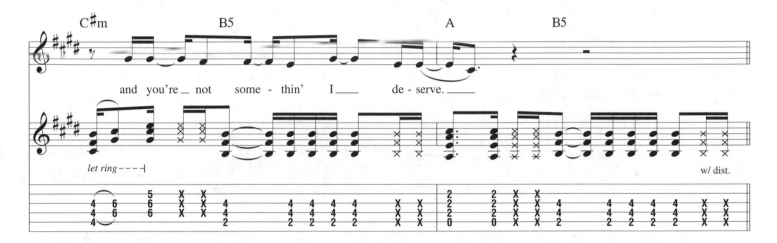

In my ___ head, ___ there's on - ly you ___ now. ___

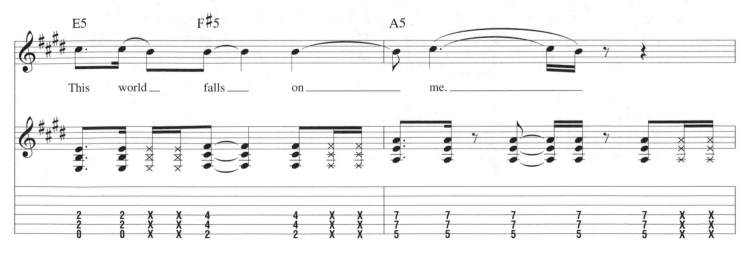

This world ___ falls ___ on ___ me. ___

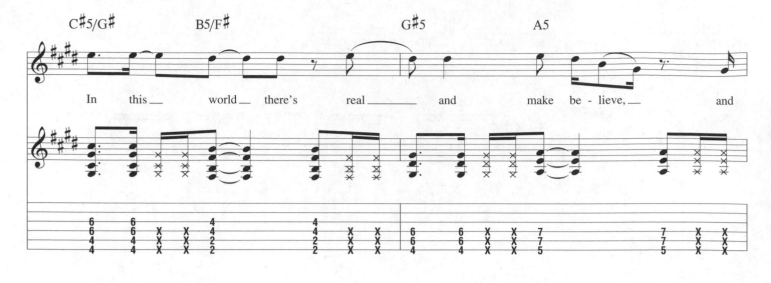

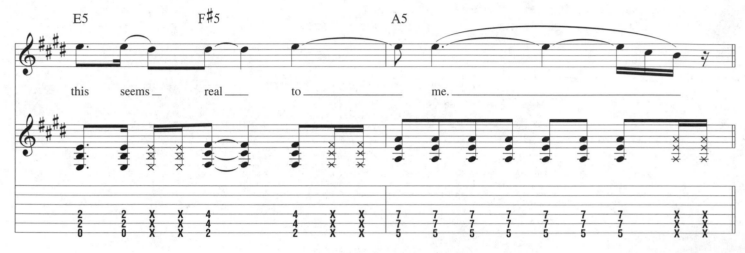

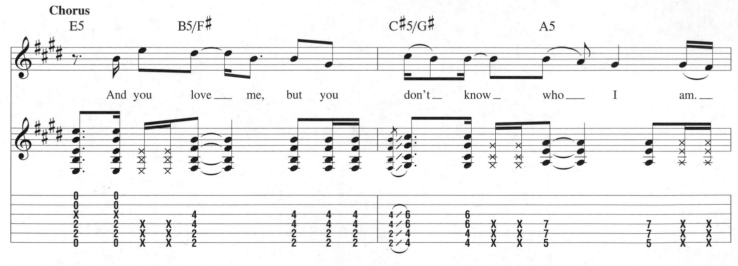

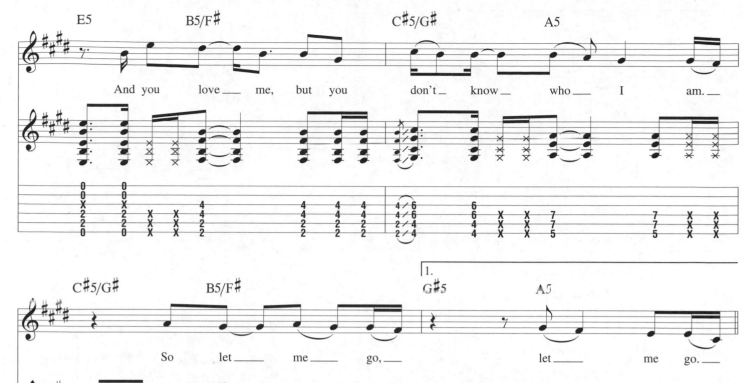

And you love __ me, but you don't __ know __ who __ I am. __

So let __ me __ go, __ let __ me go. __

dist. off

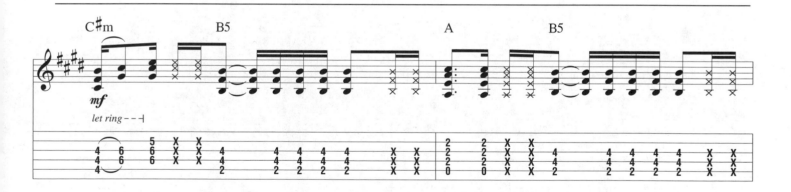

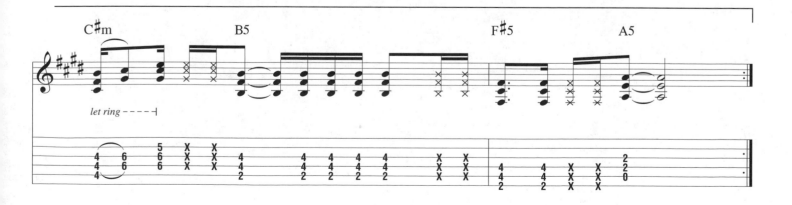

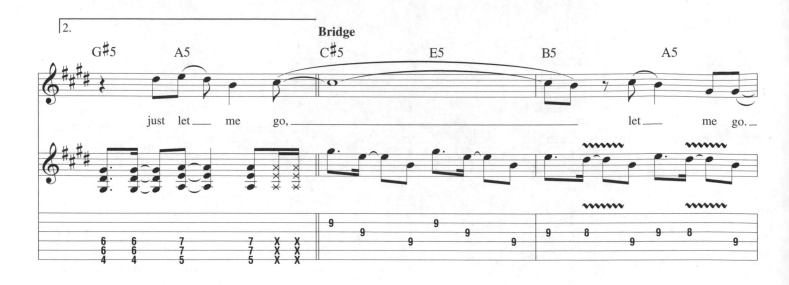

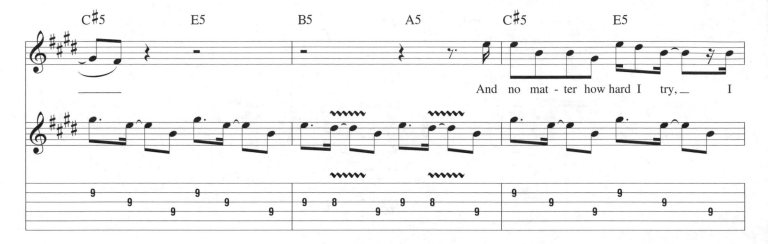

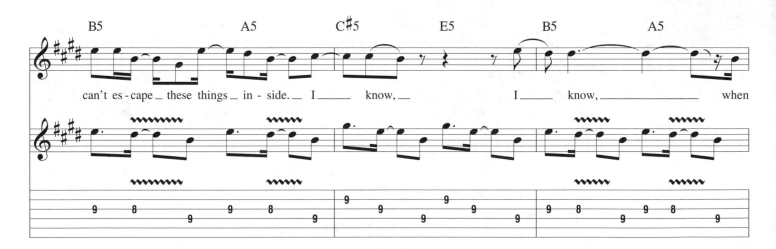

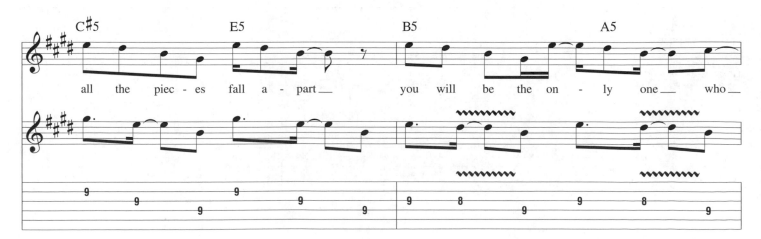

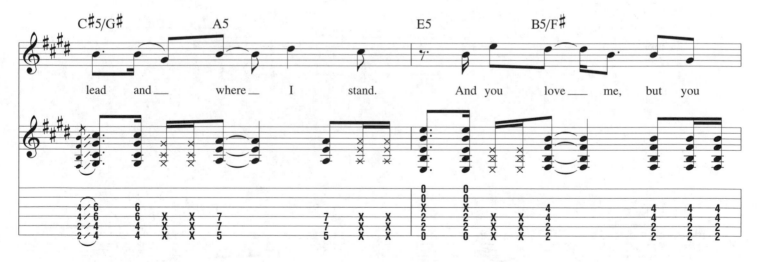

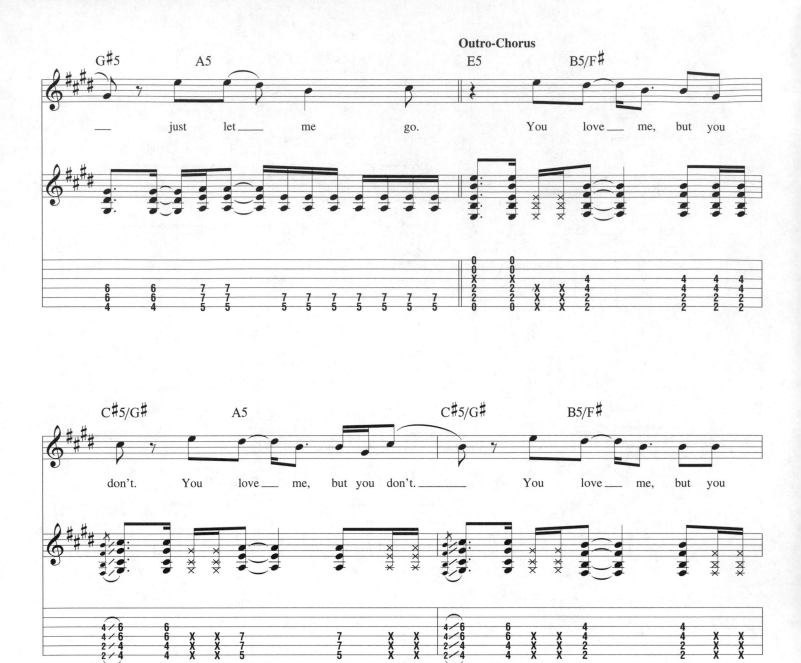

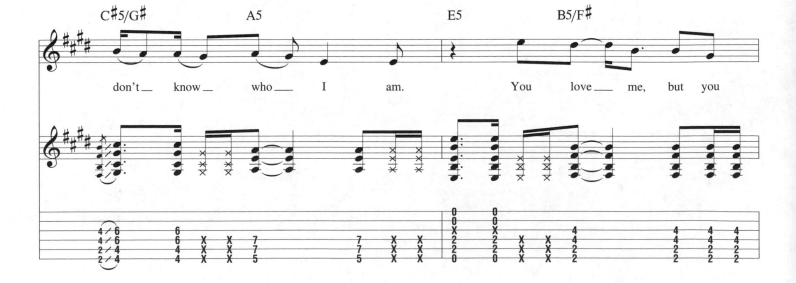

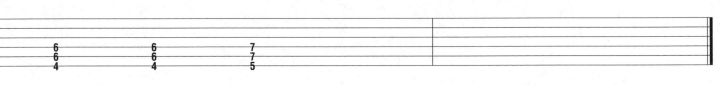

Additional Lyrics

2. I dream ahead to what I hope for,
   And I turn my back on lovin' you.
   How can this love be a good thing?
   And I know what I'm goin' through.

Live for Today

Words and Music by Brad Arnold, Robert Harrell, Christopher Henderson and Matthew Roberts

Drop D tuning:
(low to high) D-A-D-G-B-E

Intro
Moderately ♩ = 102

Verse

1. Show me the road ___ and I will

2. *See additional lyrics*

mf

dist. off
let ring throughout

find my ___ own. ___

You build your bridg - es and I'll

44

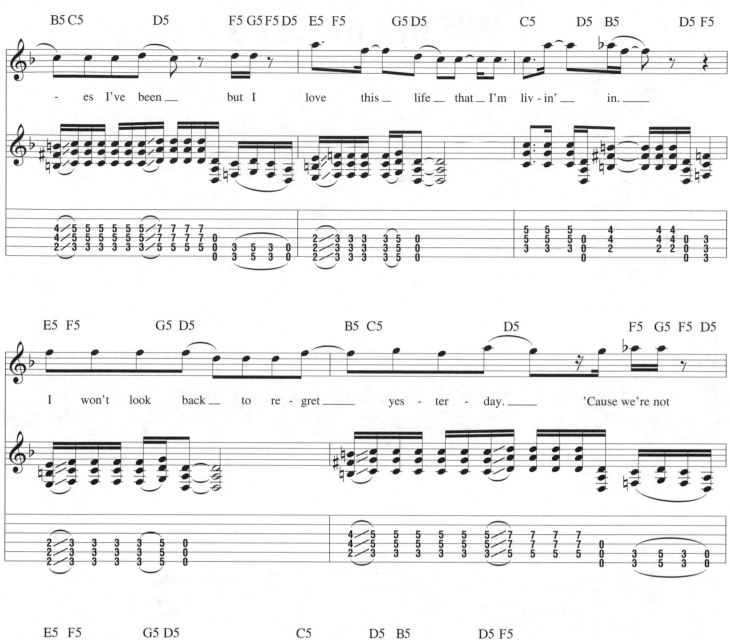

-es I've been __ but I love this __ life __ that __ I'm liv-in' __ in. __

I won't look back __ to re-gret __ yes-ter-day. __ 'Cause we're not

hand-ed to-mor-row, so I'll live for to-day. __

Additional Lyrics

2. Another day and yet another's done,
   Spending life living within the past.
   I'll take the chance before the chance has gone,
   You never know when it may be your last.

When I'm Gone

Words and Music by Matt Roberts, Brad Arnold, Christopher Henderson and Robert Harrell

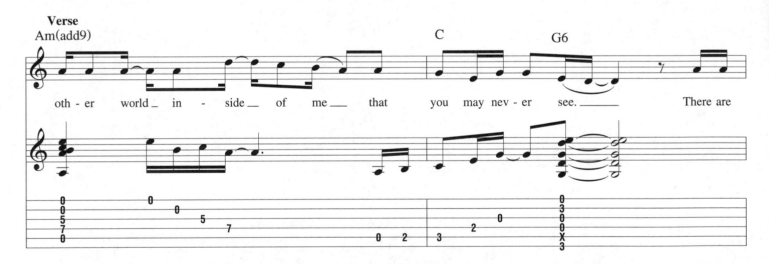

3rd time, substitute Fill 1

here, ___ right me when I'm ___ wrong. ___ Hold me when I'm scared, and love me when I'm ___ gone. ___ Ev-'ry-thing I

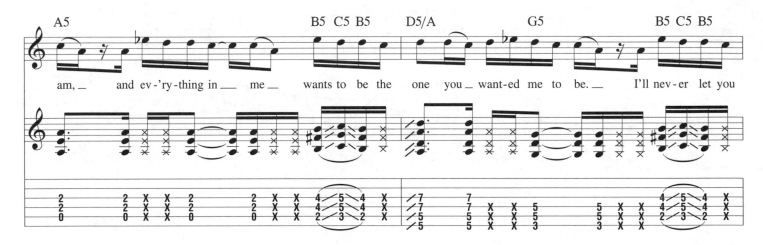

am, ___ and ev-'ry-thing in ___ me ___ wants to be the one you ___ want-ed me to be. ___ I'll nev-er let you

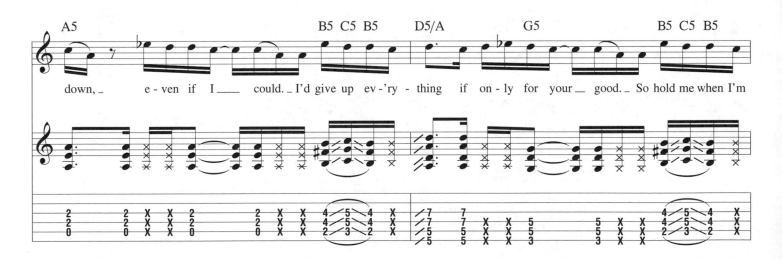

down, ___ e - ven if I ___ could. ___ I'd give up ev-'ry - thing if on - ly for your ___ good. ___ So hold me when I'm

Fill 1

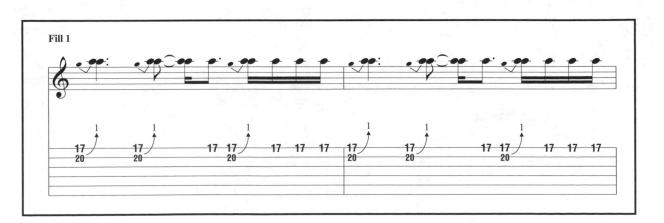

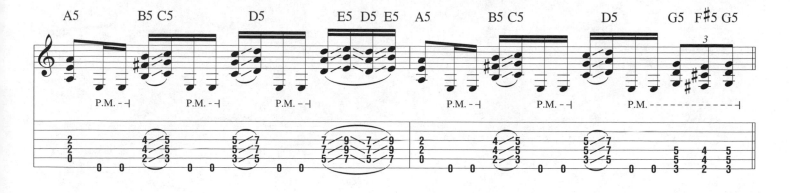

Interlude

May - be I'm__ just blind.__

Guitar Solo

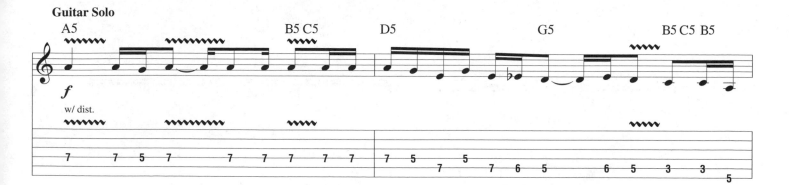

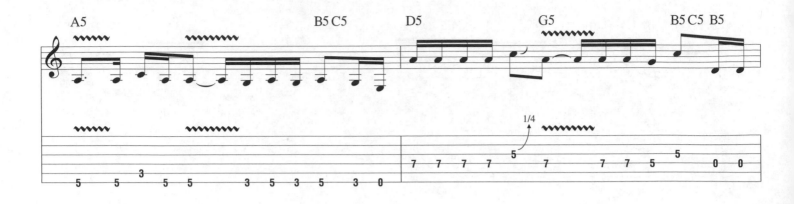

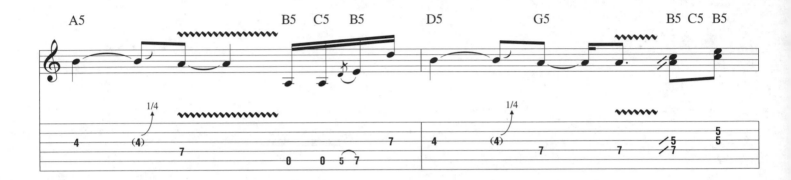

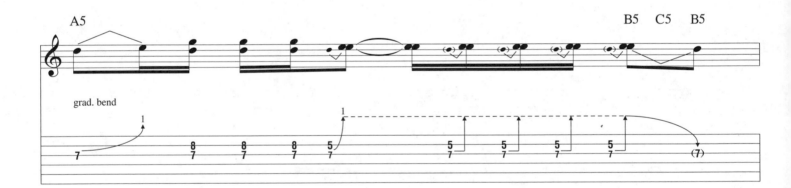

D.S. al Coda 2

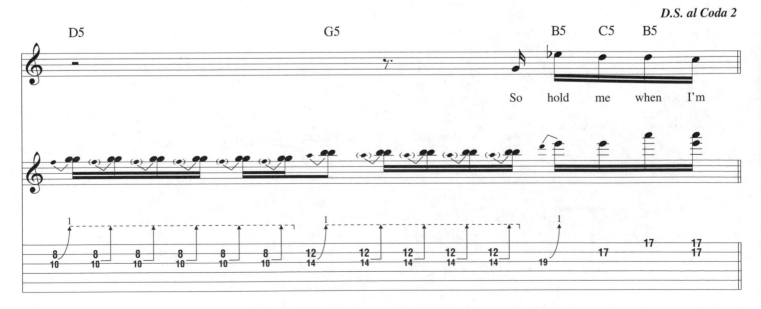

So   hold   me   when   I'm

⊕ Coda 2

Outro

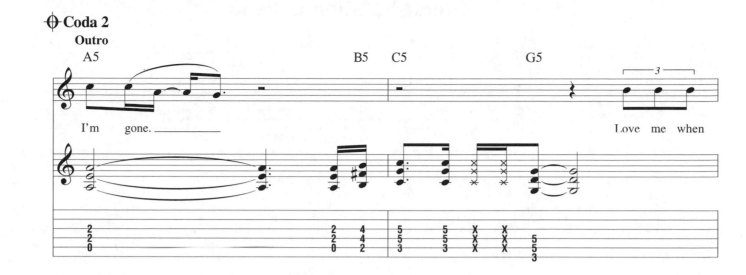

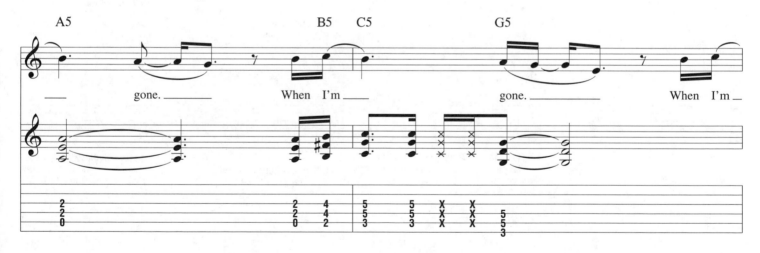

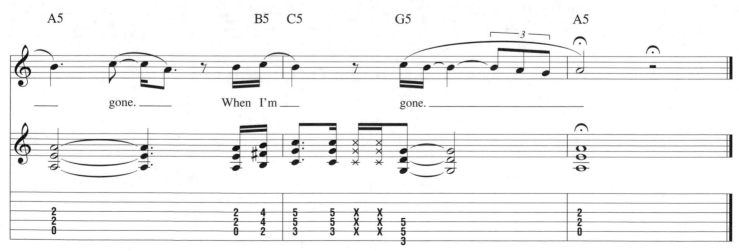

Guitar Notation Legend

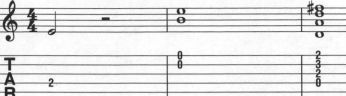

THE MUSICAL STAFF shows pitches and rhythms and is divided by bar lines into measures. Pitches are named after the first seven letters of the alphabet.

TABLATURE graphically represents the guitar fingerboard. Each horizontal line represents a string, and each number represents a fret.

4th string, 2nd fret   1st & 2nd strings open, played together   open D chord

HALF-STEP BEND: Strike the note and bend up 1/2 step.

WHOLE-STEP BEND: Strike the note and bend up one step.

GRACE NOTE BEND: Strike the note and bend up as indicated. The first note does not take up any time.

SLIGHT (MICROTONE) BEND: Strike the note and bend up 1/4 step.

BEND AND RELEASE: Strike the note and bend up as indicated, then release back to the original note. Only the first note is struck.

PRE-BEND: Bend the note as indicated, then strike it.

VIBRATO: The string is vibrated by rapidly bending and releasing the note with the fretting hand.

PALM MUTING: The note is partially muted by the pick hand lightly touching the string(s) just before the bridge.

HAMMER-ON: Strike the first (lower) note with one finger, then sound the higher note (on the same string) with another finger by fretting it without picking.

PULL-OFF: Place both fingers on the notes to be sounded. Strike the first note and without picking, pull the finger off to sound the second (lower) note.

LEGATO SLIDE: Strike the first note and then slide the same fret-hand finger up or down to the second note. The second note is not struck.

SHIFT SLIDE: Same as legato slide, except the second note is struck.

TRILL: Very rapidly alternate between the notes indicated by continuously hammering on and pulling off.

TAPPING: Hammer ("tap") the fret indicated with the pick-hand index or middle finger and pull off to the note fretted by the fret hand.

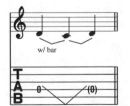

NATURAL HARMONIC: Strike the note while the fret-hand lightly touches the string directly over the fret indicated.

PINCH HARMONIC: The note is fretted normally and a harmonic is produced by adding the edge of the thumb or the tip of the index finger of the pick hand to the normal pick attack.

TREMOLO PICKING: The note is picked as rapidly and continuously as possible.

VIBRATO BAR DIVE AND RETURN: The pitch of the note or chord is dropped a specified number of steps (in rhythm) then returned to the original pitch.

VIBRATO BAR SCOOP: Depress the bar just before striking the note, then quickly release the bar.

VIBRATO BAR DIP: Strike the note and then immediately drop a specified number of steps, then release back to the original pitch.

Additional Musical Definitions

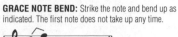

(accent) • Accentuate note (play it louder)

(staccato) • Play the note short

D.S. al Coda • Go back to the sign (𝄋), then play until the measure marked **"To Coda"**, then skip to the section labelled **"Coda."**

D.C. al Fine • Go back to the beginning of the song and play until the measure marked **"Fine"** (end).

Fill • Label used to identify a brief melodic figure which is to be inserted into the arrangement.

N.C. • No Chord

• Repeat measures between signs.

1. **2.** • When a repeated section has different endings, play the first ending only the first time and the second ending only the second time.